Hiking Free

Allergy Friendly Recipes For The Outdoors

110+ Recipes That Are Top 8 Allergen Free: No Gluten, Peanut, Tree Nuts, Soy, Seafood/Shellfish, Dairy & Egg

By Sarah Kirkconnell

www.trailcooking.com

Hiking Free

Published by Bay Street Publishing, a part of Bay Street Communications, LLC.

Copyright © 2018 By Sarah Kirkconnell and Matthew Kirkconnell

All rights reserved. No part of this publication may be reproduced in any form, or by any electronic, mechanical, including photocopying, recording or any information storage and retrieval system, without express written permission from the publisher, except for use in reviews.

Trademarks:

All terms mentioned in this book that are known to be trademarks or service marks have been appropriately capitalized. Bay Street Publishing cannot attest to the accuracy of this information. Use of a term in the book should not be regarded as affecting the validity of any trademark or service mark.

Warranty and Disclaimer:

The information in this book is distributed on an "as is" basis, without warranty. Although every precaution has been taken in the preparation of this work, neither the author(s) nor the publisher shall have any liability or responsibility to any person or entity with respect to any loss or damage caused or alleged to be caused directly or indirectly by the information contained in this work. The publisher and author take no responsibility for the use of any materials or methods described in this book, nor any products thereof. Neither the author(s) nor the publisher are offering medical advice.

Other Information:

Cover Design by Sarah Kirkconnell

Cover and interior photography by Sarah Kirkconnell

First Edition: January 2018

The Back Story

There was a time when I had no fears over what to bring with us on backpacking trips. That changed when our youngest son, Alistaire, came along. He was diagnosed with multiple severe food allergies not long after his first birthday. It affected our getting out to hike until I became comfortable with different methods of cooking, and many new foods. Slowly it became our new normal at home, and I was able to let go of the fear.

We wanted to bring to others what has worked for us. Whether it is for you, or for someone else, we want our readers to feel they can still be in the outdoors when common outdoor food is a poison to them. If you are like our family, you know that most of your food has to come from safe sources, and commercially made meals are nearly always not safe to take along, due to cross-contamination.

Top 8 Allergen Free: No Gluten, Peanut, Tree Nuts, Soy, Seafood/Shellfish, Dairy & Egg. Because legume allergies often run with peanut, the recipes are free of them as well. With other potential allergens such as corn, soy, sunflower and so on, we offer options to work with it. For example, Alistaire developed both a sunflower and a soy allergy when he was 4. We learned options and kept going on. However, if they are items you can eat, enjoy!

Cooking & Gear Methods

Cooking Methods

When we first started writing recipes for the outdoors, our goal was to make the recipes easy for everyone. In 2004 when I started writing and recipe development, we took the method of "bag meals" and turned it into FBC (Freezer Bag Cooking). In those days only a handful of recipes existed, but with a lot of free time for backpacking, we came up with thousands of recipes. I branched out into one pot meals, and sometimes gourmet meals that required multiple pots. I wasn't set in my ways, it was all fun!

Based on feedback from readers with allergies, we found one pot meals, made in a trusted pot, was the most popular cooking method, so we based the majority of the recipes in this book on that method.

Tips On Cooking:

When hiking at higher altitudes, or in cooler temperatures, many of the recipes will cook better if you wrap your cooking vessel in a pot cozy. This can be a dedicated gear item (they are easy to make) or you can can use other items you have on hand (though always use a dedicated cozy if you hike in bear territory and never clothing).

Food Substitutions:

With different allergies, especially lesser occurring ones, it can be hard to find recipes that work. In many cases, swapping out is easy on key ingredients.

Powdered coconut milk = dry rice milk (find on Amazon)
Coconut oil = olive or avocado oil
Sunflower seeds = hulled hemp seeds or chopped up pumpkin seeds
Seed butter = Instead of sunflower, use pumpkin butter or coconut butter
White rice = brown rice or multi grain instant (a mix of rice and quinoa)

Packages To Read:

Carefully read labels on canned chicken. Not all brands are gluten-free, and some have a much cleaner ingredient list. Preferably, organic is best.

Natural shelf stable bacon can be found in higher end stores.

Broth concentrate sticks. Most brands have a short, and gluten-free, ingredient list. Find a DIY dry bouillon recipe in the Dry Mixes section.

Powdered coconut milk is easily sourced on Amazon. Read carefully, as 'coconut cream powder', which is different, often has lactose in it. Creamed coconut, which comes in bars, and is grated, can be used as well.

Gear

Buy brand name cooking pots, for best construction and performance. Cheaply made cooking pots can heat up quickly and scorch food, which in gluten-free foods, are often more delicate.

Avoid uncoated aluminium pots. They impart a bad flavor to food, but also are hard to clean.

Titanium pots are a wonderful thing when you pick them up: light as can be. However, they are poor at conducting heat, and heat up quickly. Uncoated Titanium is often hard to clean up if food burns on. They are also the most expensive choice.

Hard Anodized Aluminium (HAA) is a great middle of the road choice. It is naturally (mostly) non-stick, heats evenly and isn't expensive. It is also a lot easier to cleanup.

The easiest to use is HAA, Titanium, or aluminum coated with non-stick lining. However, no matter what is claimed by the manufacturers, you have to be careful with the lining. No metal utensils, and watch the heat, so you don't fry the lining out. Personally, I do not use non-stick with Alistaire, and we use HAA.

For safety, all food should be prepared in one specific pot, not used for anyone else, with a dedicated spoon or fork, and having your own clean up system. This can lead to arguments with hiking partners, who are used to a "group" mentality (where only 1 or 2 stoves and pots are carried, and dishwashing is passed around nightly). If they cannot accept that, you might also have to consider if they will bring potential allergen food along as well.

The Recipes

Drinks

Sarah's Hot Cocoa Master Mix

1 cup powdered coconut milk
1/4 cup cocoa powder
1/2 cup sugar
Pinch sea salt

Directions:

Mix all ingredients together and store in an airtight container or bag.

Here are a few variations to the master recipe:

Spiced Hot Cocoa Mix

Add into master mix:

1 tsp ground cardamom
1 tsp cinnamon
1 tsp ginger
1/2 tsp nutmeg

Mocha Mix

Add into master mix:

2 Tbsp instant espresso powder

To prepare any of the versions:

Add 1 cup boiling water to 1/4 cup dry mix. Stir till dissolved.

Makes about 7 servings

In Your Face Morning Mochas

1 1/4 cups powdered coconut milk
1 cup powdered sugar
1/2 cup cocoa powder
2 to 4 Tbsp instant espresso powder
1 tsp cornstarch
Pinch of salt

Mix together in a large bowl. Bag the powder into 1/2 cup portions. This should make about 6 servings.

2 Tbsp of espresso powder will provide a sweet mocha flavor, 4 Tbsp will give you the "bite" of a double shot.

*To avoid corn, use organic powdered sugar made with tapioca starch. Use tapioca starch or arrowroot instead of cornstarch.

Makes 5 to 6 servings

To prepare:

Add 1 cup boiling water slowly to the mix, stirring well. Sip away and wake up!

Spiced Cider Mix-in's

Add to a packet of commercial spiced cider:

1/4 tsp dried lemon or orange zest, stirred in.

1/4 tsp finely crumbled dried rosemary, let settle before drinking.

Brew a Chai flavored tea bag, stir in dry cider mix.

Trail Teas:

For the tea recipes, feel free to use whatever tea you like, be it black, green, white or any of the many herbal varieties.

If you have time in the morning you can brew up any tea mixture (herbal or otherwise), and let it steep in a quart bottle that is heat safe. When done steeping, cool the bottle off in a stream or lake. This can also be done in the evening, and allow it to chill overnight.

In the tea recipes where you are using loose herbs and or tea, we call for using cheesecloth or tea bags. This eliminates having to strain your tea before drinking. You can find in many natural food stores or online empty tea bags that you can fill yourself. Some are disposable; others are made of muslin fabric that you can reuse by rinsing out after use. You can also make your own tea bags economically by buying a box of unbleached coffee filters (the cone style, smallest size). Cut them down to size, fill up the bags, and use a sewing machine to seal the bag.

Rose Tea

1 Tbsp dried red rose petals

Also take:
1 Tbsp or 1 packet honey
1 packet True lemon

Pour near boiling water over the petals; let steep for a couple of minutes. Add the lemon and honey.

Serves 1

Notes: You can dry rose petals quite easily in season; make sure they come from bushes that have not been sprayed with chemicals. If using store bought, buy organic only, and sold as food grade.

Mint Tea

Put into cheesecloth or a tea bag:
1 tsp dried mint
1 tsp loose leaf green tea

Also take:
1 Tbsp or 1 packet honey

Pour near boiling water over the tea and let steep till desired. Sweeten to taste.

Serves 1

Note: Mint tea is good if you have an upset stomach or indigestion after dinner.

Ginger tea

1 tsp powdered ginger
1 Tbsp or 1 packet honey

Bring 1 cup water to a boil. Pour over ginger and honey and let steep for 5 minutes. Substitute diced crystallized (candied) ginger for a different taste.

Serves 1

Note: Ginger tea is good if you are feeling nauseated, run down or have stomach issues.

Spiced tea

1 1/2 tsp ground ginger
1 tsp ground cardamom
1/2 tsp ground cinnamon
1/2 tsp ground nutmeg
1/4 tsp ground cloves

Store in a small bag. Add 1/2 tsp or to taste to any cup of black or green tea when steeping.

Makes about 8 servings

Sage Tea

1 tsp dried whole leaf sage
1 packet True Lemon
1 Tbsp or 1 packet honey

Bring water to a boil. Pour over sage. Let steep for 5 minutes. Add lemon and honey to taste

Serves 1

Flowery Herbal Infusion

1 Tbsp dried food grade lavender flowers
2 Tbsp dried peppermint
1 Tbsp dried summer savory
1 Tbsp dried sweet marjoram
1 Tbsp dried whole calendula flowers

Use 2 teaspoon per 12 ounce cup or separate into 9 zip top bags.

Pour near boiling water over the herbs and let steep 3 to 5 minutes.
Sweeten to taste.
Herbs can be put into tea bags or cheesecloth, if desired.

Makes 9 servings

Lavender Tea

1 tsp dried food grade lavender flowers
2 tsp dried mint leaves
1 Tbsp or 1 packet honey

Pour boiling water over the herbs; let steep for 5 minutes. The amount of water is up to your cup/mug size, 8 to 12 ounces. Strain, if desired, and serve hot. Sweeten to taste.

Serves 1

Note: This can also be made as iced tea, double the herbs and let steep in 1 quart of water.

Herbal Green Tea

1 tsp loose green tea leaves
1 tsp dried crumbled rosemary leaves
1/8 tsp ground nutmeg

Put all ingredients in a tea bag or cheesecloth and steep in near boiling water for 5 minutes. (8 to 12 ounce mug) Sweeten with honey, if desired, to taste.

Serves 1

Chai Tea

1 Chai flavor black tea bag
1 Tbsp powdered coconut milk
1 Tbsp or 1 packet honey

Pour boiling water over the tea bag and let steep till ready. Add in coconut milk and honey to taste.

Serves 1

Hibiscus Tea

2 to 5 dried hibiscus flowers (find in ethnic and natural food stores)
Sugar or honey to taste

Place flowers in cup, cover with boiling water. Let steep till cool enough to drink. Sweeten if desired.

Serves 1

Note: This tea is good with powdered coconut milk added, producing a smooth tea, which is perfect for a nighttime drink. Stir in 1 to 2 Tablespoons powdered coconut milk before drinking.

Spicy Morning Tea

1/4 cup dried food grade lavender flowers
1/4 cup dried mint
1/4 cup dried rosemary leaves
2 Tbsp dried chamomile
2 Tbsp dried whole cloves

Combine all the ingredients. Store in a sealed bag or separate into 12 smaller bags.

Use 4 tsp of the mix per 12 ounces of boiling water, using cheesecloth or tea bag to hold tea. Let steep for 5 minutes. Sweeten to taste.

Makes 12 servings

Two Flower Tea

1 tsp dried food grade lavender flowers
1 tsp dried chamomile
1 tsp loose leaf green tea

Combine in cheesecloth or tea bag.

To serve, cover with near boiling water and steep for 5 minutes. Sweeten to taste.

Serves 1

Sun Tea:

Before you leave camp in the morning, fill a quart bottle with purified water and add your tea mixture. Clip it to your pack and as you walk during the day, your tea will brew. In camp tuck the bottle into a stream or lake to chill for dinner.

Sun Tea Lemonade

After brewing a quart of tea (herbal, black or green) add:
4 Tbsp lemon juice (1 large lemon)
2 Tbsp or 2 packets honey

Shake well.

Note:
If making at home before leaving for a hike, make a double batch of tea and freeze part of it as ice cubes, add to the drink before leaving, it will keep your drink cold and not get diluted tasting.

Flavors 1 quart

Trail Lemonade

In a quart water bottle:

4 packets True Lemon©, 2 Tbsp lemon juice or 1 small lemon
1 Tbsp or 1 packet honey

Directions:

Combine the lemon juice and honey. Stir 1 cup cold water into it slowly.

Serves 1

Note: Use hot water instead for a hot lemon toddy.

Maple Lemonade

In a quart water bottle:

8 packets True Lemon©, 1/4 cup lemon juice or 1 lemon
3 Tbsp pure maple syrup

Directions:

Shake gently to combine. Add 1 quart cold filtered water. Put on cap tightly and shake for a minute.

Makes 1 quart

Maple Sugar Lemonade

In a quart water bottle:

8 packets True Lemon©, 1/4 cup lemon juice or 1 lemon
3 Tbsp maple sugar

Directions:

Add 1 quart cold filtered water. Put on cap tightly and shake till sugar dissolves.

Makes 1 quart

Mocha Shake

In a sandwich bag:

1/2 cup powdered coconut milk
1 Tbsp unsweetened cocoa powder
1 Tbsp sugar
1 tsp instant espresso or coffee

Directions:

Add 1 cup cold water, seal tightly and shake till dissolved and frothed up.

In an area with clean snow? Add a little in for an extra treat!

Serves 1

Breakfast

Cranberry Orange Cereal

In a sandwich bag:

1/2 cup + 2 Tbsp cornmeal
1/4 cup dried cranberries
1 Tbsp powdered coconut milk
1 tsp brown sugar
1/4 tsp cinnamon
1/4 tsp dried diced orange peel
Pinch sea salt
2 packets True® Orange© powder or 1 tsp orange drink mix

Directions:

Bring 1 3/4 cups water to a boil.

Lower the flame to low, add in the dry ingredients and stir well with a whisk for a couple minutes.

Turn off the heat and let sit till cool enough to eat.

Serves 2

Maple Currant Cereal

In a sandwich bag:

1/2 cup + 2 Tbsp cornmeal
1 Tbsp maple sugar
1 Tbsp dried currants
1 Tbsp powdered coconut milk
Pinch sea salt

Directions:

Bring 1 1/2 cups water to a boil.

Turn the flame to low, add in the dry ingredients and stir well with a whisk for a couple minutes.

Turn off the heat and let sit until cool enough to eat.

Serves 2

Notes: While dried currants are called for in this recipe, you can substitute your choice of dried or fresh fruit. My favorite is picking fresh huckleberries along the trail when in season. If you cannot find maple sugar, you can use maple syrup or brown sugar instead.

Apricots and Coconut Cream Cereal

In a sandwich bag:

1/2 cup + 2 Tbsp cornmeal
2 Tbsp sugar
2 Tbsp coconut cream powder
2 Tbsp diced dried apricots
Pinch sea salt

Directions:

Bring 1 1/2 cups water to a boil.

Turn the flame down to low, add in the dry ingredients and stir well with a whisk for a couple minutes.

Turn off the heat and let sit until cool enough to eat.

Serves 2

Instant Oatmeal Packets

Old-fashioned oats
Quick cooking oats
Fine Sea salt

Add 1/2 cup old-fashioned oats at a time in a blender or mini food processor and blend on high until broken apart and somewhat powdery. Set aside in a small bowl, and repeat procedure if you are making a bigger batch.

In each sandwich bag:

1/4 cup quick cooking oats
2 Tbsp powdered oats
1 Tbsp soy, rice or coconut milk powder
1/8 tsp fine sea salt (if desired)

Directions:

Bring 3/4 cup water to a boil, take off the heat and add in the dry ingredients. Stir well, cover tightly and let sit for a couple minutes.

Variations:

Apple Cinnamon Oatmeal:
1 Tbsp sugar, 1/4 tsp cinnamon and 2 Tbsp diced dried apples

Sweetened Oatmeal:
1 Tbsp sugar

Brown Sugar and Cinnamon Oatmeal:
1 Tbsp brown sugar and 1/4 tsp cinnamon

Raisins and Brown Sugar Oatmeal:
1 Tbsp packed brown sugar and 1 Tbsp raisins

Peaches and Cream Oatmeal:
2 Tbsp diced dried peaches

S'More Oatmeal:
6 miniature marshmallows and 1 Tbsp chocolate chips.

Pears and Vanilla Oatmeal

In a sandwich bag:

2 packets plain instant oatmeal
2 Tbsp freeze dried or dehydrated pears, diced
1 tsp vanilla powder
1 tsp maple sugar

Directions:

Bring 1 cup water to boil in your pot. Turn the stove off and add in the dry ingredients. Stir well and let sit for a couple minutes to cool.

Serves 1

Blueberry and Lemon Oatmeal

In a sandwich bag:

2 packets instant plain oatmeal
1 tsp dried lemon zest
1/4 cup dried blueberries
1 Tbsp brown sugar
1 tsp vanilla powder

Also take 1 Tbsp or 1 packet honey

Directions:

BrIng 1 cup water to a boil in your pot. Turn off the stove, add in the honey and dry ingredients and stir well. Let sit till cool enough to eat.

Serves 1

Lazy Morning Oatmeal

In a sandwich bag:

2 cups quick-cooking oats

In a sandwich bag:

3/4 cup freeze-dried or dried apricots, chopped
2 Tbsp shredded coconut
1/3 cup powdered coconut milk
2 Tbsp honey powder or 2 Tbsp honey

Directions:

Bring 5 cups water and the apricot bag ingredients to a boil in your pot. Add in the oats, return to a boil and simmer on lowered heat for 1 minute or till the thickness you like.

Serves 2 to 3

Brown Sugar & Sunflower Oats

Pack in a sandwich bag:

1 cup quick-cooking oats
1/4 cup powdered coconut milk
2 Tbsp raisins or diced dried fruit/berries
2 Tbsp brown sugar
1 tsp ground cinnamon

Also take:

1 packet/tub Sunbutter Sunflower Seed Spread

Directions:

Bring 2 cups water to boil, add in dry ingredients, stirring well. Take off heat and let rest for a minute. Stir in sunflower butter.

Serves 2.

Notes:

To serve two easily, carry an extra quart freezer bag. Cuff down to make a "bowl", divide oatmeal and enjoy.

Carrot Cake In A Bowl

Ingredients:

1/2 cup rolled oats
2 Tbsp diced dried carrots
3 Tbsp brown sugar
2 Tbsp raisins
2 Tbsp powdered coconut milk
¼ tsp ground cinnamon
Pinch fine sea salt
2 Tbsp shredded coconut

At home:

Whirl the oats in a blender until about ⅓ of the original size. Put them in a sandwich bag. Process the carrots in the same manner, adding them to the bag along with the other dry ingredients.

In camp:

Bring 1 1/4 cups water to a boil in your pot. Add in the dry ingredients; stirring well and let come back to a boil.

Take off the stove, cover tightly and let sit for 5 minutes. Stir well and top with coconut.

Tropical Oatmeal

In a sandwich bag:

2 packs instant plain oatmeal
2 Tbsp freeze-dried bananas
2 Tbsp freeze-dried mango
1 Tbsp brown sugar
1 Tbsp powdered coconut milk

Directions:

Bring 1 1/4 cups water to a boil in your pot. Add in the dry ingredients; stir well and let sit for a couple minutes to cool down.

Serves 1

Note:

Mango can be a similar allergy if a cashew allergy exists. Substitute dried papaya or apricots instead.

Leftover Oatmeal Cakes

So let's say you make up oatmeal and either you made too much or no one wants it, what to do with it? Fry it up!

Leftover cooked oatmeal, cooled
Coconut or olive oil
Maple syrup
Jam or Jelly packets
Seed butter packets

Before moving on for the day take the cold oatmeal and cut or scoop out into portions. In a fry pan lid, heat up a Tbsp of oil over a low flame. Drop the oatmeal in and fry till golden brown, flipping over once.

Serve with syrup, jam and or seed butter on top.

Makes as many as the leftovers you have!

Brown Sugar & Cinnamon Quinoa

In a sandwich bag:

1/3 cup instant quinoa flakes
1 1/2 Tbsp brown sugar
1/4 tsp ground cinnamon

Directions:

Bring 1 cup water to a boil in your pot, add in dry ingredients. Cook over a low flame for 90 seconds, stirring constantly.

Notes:

Find instant quinoa flakes in natural food stores. Substitute in cooked and dehydrated quinoa, lightly buzzed in a blender.

Coconut Fruit Rice

In a sandwich bag:

1 1/2 cups instant rice
1/2 tsp cinnamon
2 Tbsp powdered coconut milk
1 Tbsp shredded coconut
1 Tbsp hemp seeds
1 Tbsp brown sugar
Pinch sea salt

In a sandwich bag:

1/4 cup diced dried fruit of choice

Also take:

2 Tbsp or 2 packets coconut oil
1 packet honey

Directions:

Cover the dried fruit with water and let sit for 10 minutes. Drain well, reserving water.
At the same time, melt coconut oil over medium flame in your pot. Add in the fruit and let sauté for a minute.

Add water to the reserved soaking water, to make 1 1/2 cups, add to the pot and bring to a boil. Add the dry ingredients and stir well. Turn off the stove and let sit for 10 minutes.

Fluff with fork and drizzle the honey over.

Serves 2

Cherry and Hemp Breakfast Rice

Pack in snack bag:

1/2 cup instant white rice
1/4 cup dried cherries
1/4 cup dry coconut milk powder
1/2 tsp ground cinnamon
Pinch sea salt

Also take:

3 date nectar or honey sticks
1 Tbsp hemp seeds, in a small bag

Directions:

Bring 1/2 cup + 2 Tbsp water to a boil in a small pot with 2 sticks worth of the date nectar or honey. Add in dry ingredients, stir and cover. Take off heat and let sit for 10 minutes.

Stir well, top with hemp seeds and remaining stick of sweetener.

Serves 1.

Quinoa Granola

1/2 cup raw quinoa
1/2 cup rolled oats
2 Tbsp hemp seeds
1/8 tsp fine sea salt
2 Tbsp honey or maple syrup
2 Tbsp raisins or dried cranberries

At home:

Preheat your oven to 225*. Rinse the quinoa and shake dry. In a medium pot add the quinoa and cover with water. Bring to a boil and cook for 7 minutes. Take off the stove, drain and rinse with cold water.

Combine everything, but the raisins, on an ungreased cookie sheet and place in the oven. Check every 10 minutes and stir often with a silicone spatula so it toasts evenly. Cook until dry and lightly toasted, about 45 minutes. Mix in the raisins and let cool. Once cool store in an airtight container or plastic storage bag.

For trail:

Pack how much granola you like to eat in a sandwich bag. To serve, sprinkle 2 Tbsp coconut, rice, or soy milk powder in the bag along with 1 cup water. Stir well and serve.

Servings depend on appetite.

Apple Sunflower Granola

Ingredients:

3 cups rolled oats
1 cup raw sunflower seeds, ground
6 Tbsp sunflower oil
6 Tbsp pure maple syrup
1 tsp ground cinnamon
1/4 tsp fine sea salt
1 cup dried apples, chopped

Directions:

Preheat oven to 300°.

Mix oil, maple syrup, cinnamon, and salt in a small bowl.

Put oats and sunflower seeds in a large mixing bowl, pour oil mixture over, stir to coat. Spread on a rimmed baking sheet.

Bake for 40 minutes, stirring halfway through.

Let cool fully on counter, stirring a few times, to break up granola. When cool, stir in apple pieces.

Store in an airtight container. Use within a week or two for best taste, especially in high humidity.

Makes about 5 cups.

Notes:

Use hemp seed for the sunflowers, if there is an allergy. Avocado or coconut oil can be used for the sunflower oil.

Spicy Hash Browns

In a quart freezer bag:

1 1/4 cups instant hash browns
2 Tbsp diced dried bell peppers
1/4 to 1/2 tsp diced dried jalapeños
1 tsp onion powder
1/2 tsp granulated garlic
1/2 tsp ground cumin
1/2 tsp ground coriander
1/4 tsp fine sea salt
1/4 tsp ground black pepper

Also take:

2 Tbsp or 2 packets olive oil

Directions:

Add 1 1/2 cups very warm water to the bag, seal tightly and let sit covered for at least 30 minutes to rehydrate.

Heat the oil in a wide 2 liter pot over a medium flame, add in the hash browns and cook till crispy and golden brown, stirring as needed.

Serve with ketchup or salsa if desired.

Serves 2

Notes:

Dried jalapeños have quite the kick, so use the lower end if you do not like as much heat. To make more filling consider adding in 1/2 cup freeze-dried sausage with the hash browns. Add an additional 1/2 cup water and let rehydrate as noted.

Sausage Grits

In a sandwich bag:

2 packets plain instant grits
1 tsp diced dried onions
1/4 tsp ground black pepper

Also take:

1 stick shelf stable sausage
1 Tbsp or 1 packet olive oil

Directions:

Dice the sausage up.

In your pot bring 1 cup water to a boil. Add in the sausage and dry ingredients and stir well. Turn off the stove and cover tightly, letting sit for 5 minutes.

Serves 1

Maple Bacon Grits

In a sandwich bag:

2 packets instant plain grits
1/4 cup powdered coconut milk
2 Tbsp maple or coconut sugar
2 Tbsp crumbled shelf stable bacon
1 Tbsp hemp seeds

Directions:

Bring 1 cup water to a boil in your pot. Add in the dry ingredients; stir well and let sit for a couple minutes to cool down.

Serves 1

Cranberry Sunshine Grits

In a sandwich bag:

2 packets instant plain grits
1/4 cup dried cranberries
1 Tbsp powdered coconut milk
1 tsp brown sugar
1/4 tsp ground cinnamon
2 packets True® Orange powder

Directions:

Bring 1 cup + 2 Tbsp water to a boil in your pot. Add in the dry ingredients; stir well and let sit for a couple minutes to cool down.

Serves 1

Maple Currant Grits

In a sandwich bag:

2 packets instant plain grits
1 Tbsp maple or coconut sugar
1 Tbsp dried currants
1 Tbsp powdered coconut milk

Directions:

Bring 1 cup water to a boil in your pot. Add in the dry ingredients; stir well and let sit for a couple minutes to cool down.

Serves 1

Notes: While dried currants are called for, you can substitute raisins, dried cranberries or even better, fresh huckleberries in season.

Seed Butter & Honey Granola Wraps

Bring with you per wrap:

1 large gluten-free flour tortilla
1 ounce or packet seed butter of choice
1 packet honey
2 Tbsp granola of choice

Directions:

Spread the seed butter on the tortilla, drizzle the honey on top. Sprinkle with the granola, and roll up.

Serves 1

Lunch

Seed Spread

1/2 cup sunflower, pumpkin or hemp butter
1/4 cup powdered coconut milk
1/4 cup molasses
1 Tbsp honey
1/4 tsp ground cinnamon

Directions:

Mix well and store in a plastic tub.

Eat by the spoonful or serve on your favorite cracker, gluten-free tortilla or bread.

Apples and Twigs

1 apple
1 packet or 1 to 2 tablespoons seed butter
2 Tbsp allergy safe granola
2 Tbsp dairy-free mini chocolate chips

Directions:

At home pack the granola and chocolate chips in a snack bag.

For a backpacking trip, pack the apple into a cup or mug to protect. For day trips, slice your apple and toss with a little fresh lemon juice to prevent browning, then pack in a small bag. Tuck the seed butter packet in with it. For ease in preparing, pack a small sheet of parchment paper to work on.

On trail:

Slice the apple up (if not already sliced) and lay on the parchment paper. Spread the seed butter evenly on. Dip the slices in the granola bag, then enjoy!

Notes:

For best results use a small sized granola or run it through a blender to make small.
You can also make one slice up, then top with another apple slice to make an apple sammie.

You can also find bags of pre-sliced apples in many grocery stores these days, in the produce department.

Harvest Chicken Salad Wraps

Ingredients:

7 ounce pouch chicken
1/4 cup diced dried apples
1/4 cup hemp seeds
2 Tbsp freeze-dried or dried sliced celery
1 Tbsp dried cranberries or golden raisins
1 Tbsp or 1 packet olive oil
2 large gluten-free flour tortillas
1 packet each salt and pepper

Directions:

At home pack the apples, cranberries and celery in a small plastic bag. Put the hemp seeds in a small bag. Pack with everything else.

Cover the celery and apples with cool water and let sit for 10-20 minutes. Drain any remaining water carefully.

Open the chicken pouch and add the vegetables, hemp seeds, and cranberries. Toss to coat. Add in olive oil, salt and pepper to taste.

Spread on the tortillas.

Homemade Granola Wraps

Ingredients:

1/4 cup apple juice
1/2 cup seed butter of choice
1/4 cup honey or maple syrup
1/2 tsp ground cinnamon
1/2 tsp pure vanilla extract
2 cups rolled oats
1/4 cup dried cranberries
1/4 cup dried prunes, diced

Directions:

Combine apple juice thru vanilla in a small saucepan, heat till seed butter is soft and blended, over medium heat.

Put oats in a medium bowl and pour sauce over, mix well.

Spread on a parchment paper lined tray and bake at 350* for 25 minutes. Stir every 5 minutes. Remove from the oven; add fruit and let cool.

Divide into four small snack size bags.

On the trail prep:

Spread 1 Tbsp of seed butter of choice on a tortilla, drizzle with 1 packet honey, and sprinkle granola on top.

Makes 4 to 8 wraps per batch depending on how much granola you like in your wrap.

Mushroom Bruschetta

At home in a non stick sauté pan, cook till golden:

12 medium mushroom caps, sliced thin in matchstick size pieces
1 Tbsp lemon juice
1 Tbsp lemon zest or 1 tsp dried lemon peel
1 Tbsp parsley, chopped
Salt and pepper, to taste, if desired

Dehydrator instructions:

Dry at 135* on a lined tray. Measure dry mix in a dry measuring cup and note on bag how much. Pack in a sandwich bag.

Take with you:

Mushroom mix
1 Tbsp or 1 packet extra virgin olive oil
Gluten-free tortillas, pitas or crackers to top

Directions:

Rehydrate using a 1:1 ratio of water to dry mix, with oil mixed in. Let sit for 15 minutes, tightly sealed, till full rehydrated. Add a bit more water of needed.

Serve with nibbelage of choice.

Makes 1 bag that serves 1 to 2

BBQ Beef Rice Burritos

In a sandwich bag:

1 cup instant rice
1 Tbsp freeze-dried ground beef or cooked and dehydrated hamburger
1 Tbsp diced dried onion

Also take:

2 gluten-free flour tortillas
2 packets BBQ sauce

Directions:

Bring 1 cup water to a boil in your pot, add in rice. Mix well, put lid on for 10 minutes.

Top tortillas with rice, squeeze the BBQ sauce on and roll up.

For a first night out dinner, take a whole avocado and slice it up while the rice cooks. Add the slices to the burritos.

Serves 1

Dinner

Soup

Spicy Beef Soup

In a snack bag:

1 Tbsp tomato powder
1 Tbsp freeze-dried beef or cooked and dehydrated hamburger
1/4 tsp dried diced garlic
1/8 tsp red pepper flakes
Couple grinds black pepper

Also take:

1 packet beef broth concentrate

Directions:

Mix with 1 cup boiling water in a mug or cup and stir well. Let sit for a couple minutes till cool enough to sip on.

Serves 1

Hot & Sour Soup

In a snack bag:

1 Tbsp finely crumbled dried mushrooms
1 tsp low sodium chicken or vegetable bouillon
1/2 tsp dried onion
1/4 tsp dried parsley
Pinch cayenne pepper

Carry in a leak proof bottle:

1 packet beef broth concentrate
1/4 tsp coconut aminos
1/2 tsp rice vinegar

Directions:

Mix with 1 cup boiling water in a mug or cup and stir well. Let sit for a couple minutes till cool enough to sip on.

Serves 1

Coconut Curry Soup

In a snack bag:

1 Tbsp powdered coconut milk
1/4 tsp curry powder
Pinch cayenne pepper

Also take:

1 packet chicken or vegetable broth concentrate

Mug method:

Mix with 1 cup boiling water in a mug or cup and stir well. Let sit for a couple minutes till cool enough to sip on.

Serves 1

Chicken Broth

In a snack bag:

1 tsp diced dried onion
1 packet True Lemon powder
1/4 tsp dried parsley
1/4 tsp granulated garlic
Couple grinds black pepper

Also take:

1 packet chicken broth concentrate

Directions:

Mix with 1 cup boiling water in a mug or cup and stir well. Let sit for a couple minutes till cool enough to sip on.

Serves 1

Bacon Potato Chowder

In a sandwich bag:

1/2 cup freeze-dried sweet corn
1/3 cup diced sun-dried tomatoes
2 Tbsp dried onion
2 Tbsp dried celery
1 Tbsp diced dried bell pepper
1 1/2 tsp dried parsley
1/2 tsp granulated sugar
1/4 tsp paprika
1/4 tsp fine sea salt
1/4 tsp ground black pepper

In a sandwich bag:

1/2 cup instant mashed potatoes
1/4 cup powdered coconut milk
1/4 cup shelf stable bacon

Directions:

In a 2 liter pot, combine 3 cups of water, and the first bag and bring to a boil.

Add in the second bag, stir well, then turn off the stove and let sit tightly covered for 5 minutes.

Serves 2

Beef Curry Noodle Bowl

In a sandwich bag:

3 ounce package rice ramen noodles, crumbled (discard flavor packet)
1/2 cup diced jerky
1/2 cup freeze-dried vegetable mix
1/4 cup raisins (or dried berry mix)
1 Tbsp mild curry powder
1/4 tsp granulated garlic

Also take:

1 packet beef broth concentrate

Directions:

Put 2 cups water in your pot, stir in all the ingredients, then bring to a boil. Let simmer for a couple minutes, turn off the stove, cover tightly and let sit for 5 minutes.

Serves 1 to 2, depending on appetite.

Creamy Tomato Soup

Process in a blender till combined:

1/2 cup diced sun-dried tomatoes
2 Tbsp powdered coconut milk
1 Tbsp tomato powder
1 Tbsp diced dried onions
1/2 tsp sugar
1/2 tsp Italian seasoning blend
1/4 tsp diced dried garlic
1/4 tsp ground black pepper
1/8 tsp fine sea salt

Pack in a pint freezer or sandwich bag, adding in 1 Tablespoon shelf stable bacon before sealing the bag.

Directions:

Add dry ingredients to 1 cup water in your pot. Bring to a boil, stirring often. Turn off the heat, cover tightly and let sit for 5 minutes.

Serves 1

Curried Chicken and Apple Soup

In a sandwich bag:

1/2 cup instant rice
1/4 cup diced dried apples
2 Tbsp diced dried onion
2 Tbsp dried celery flakes
1 Tbsp mild curry powder
1 bay leaf

Also take:

7 ounce pouch chicken
2 Tbsp powdered coconut milk
2 Tbsp or 2 packets olive oil

Directions:

Add the oil, dry ingredients (except for coconut milk), chicken and 3 cups water to a 2 liter pot.

Bring to a boil and let simmer gently for 5 minutes.

Stir in the coconut milk and heat through.

Season to taste with salt and pepper if desired.

Serves 2

Note:

Celery flakes can be found in the spice aisle. You can also use freeze-dried diced celery instead.

American Pho

In a sandwich bag:

3 ounce package rice ramen (discard seasoning packet)
2 Tbsp crumbled dried mushrooms
2 Tbsp freeze-dried vegetable mix
1 tsp diced dried onion
1 tsp dried parsley
1/4 tsp oregano
1/4 tsp granulated garlic
Pinch red pepper flakes
Ground pepper to taste

Also take:

2 to 4 tsp coconut aminos
2 packets beef broth concentrate

Directions:

Add 2 cups water, broth packets, coconut aminos, and the dry ingredients to your pot.

Bring to a boil. Turn off the heat. Cover tightly and let sit for 5 minutes.

Serves 1 as a meal, 2 as a side cup of soup.

Chicken and Apple Rice Stew

In a sandwich bag:

1 cup instant brown rice
1/3 cup diced dried apple
1/4 cup diced sun-dried tomato
1 Tbsp diced dried onion
2 tsp mild curry powder
1 tsp diced dried garlic
1 tsp dried cilantro
1 tsp dried parsley

Also take:

4 packets chicken broth concentrate
7 ounce pouch chicken

Directions:

Bring 4 cups water, chicken and the dry ingredients to a boil in your pot.

Cook for 5 minutes, stirring occasionally over low heat.

Remove from heat, seal tightly and let sit for 5 minutes. Stir well and salt to taste, if desired.

Serves 2 to 3

High Protein Broth

In a snack size bag:

1 packet plain gelatin
1 tsp onion powder
1/4 tsp granulated garlic
1/8 tsp ground black pepper

Also take:

1 packet beef broth concentrate

Directions:

Add dry mix and broth concentrate to 1 cup boiling water in a mug. Stir well and let cool enough to sip.

Serves 1

Notes:

The plain gelatin provides 8 grams of protein per packet and thickens the broth a bit as well. You can use this broth as a base for adding whatever you like or leave it as is.

If you have an evening where you are tired and dehydrated a simple cup of broth can help rehydrate you quickly.

Fuel Saver Quinoa

1/2 cup quinoa
1 cup water

Directions:

Add the quinoa and water to a small cooking pot (a 1 to 1.7 Liter works well). Add a pinch of salt if desired.

Bring to a boil and let boil for 5 minutes - keep the pot's lid on mostly and stir periodically. Lower the flame if needed.

Take off the stove, cover tightly and insulate, either with a pot cozy or what you have on hand. Let sit for 15 minutes without disturbing.

Fluff up and enjoy.

Notes:

It is very important you buy a brand of quinoa that is pre-washed. Most US sold brands are, but do look. If it doesn't say it is, pass on it!

While this recipe might seem simple an often asked question is "Can I cook quinoa on the trail without dehydrating?" It works well but you do need to keep a close eye on it while it boils.

Use this as a base and add whatever you crave: spices, herbs, lower sodium bouillon, etc.

Rice Dishes

Mexi Rice:

In a sandwich bag:

1 cup instant rice (white or brown)
1/4 cup dehydrated Pico de Gallo mix

Directions:

Bring 1 1/4 cups water to a boil in your pot. Stir in rice and Pico, cover tightly and let sit for 15 minutes. Fluff up. Salt to taste.

Serves 2 as a side dish.

Note:

Find the Pico de Gallo recipe in the dry mixes and seasoning section.

Add in 1/4 cup freeze dried beef (with 1/4 cup extra water) to make a full meal.

Chicken Curry Rice

Pack a sandwich bag:

1 cup instant rice
2 Tbsp golden raisins
2 Tbsp diced dried apples
2 tsp diced dried onion
1 tsp mild curry powder
1/8 tsp ground allspice
1/8 tsp ground cinnamon
1/8 tsp fine sea salt

Also take:

5 ounce can chicken
1 Tbsp or 1 packet olive or coconut oil

Directions:

Bring 1 cup water and chicken, with any broth, and oil, to a boil in your pot. Add in dry ingredients, stir well, cover tightly and let sit for 15 minutes.

Serves 1.

Cranberry Chicken Rice

In a sandwich bag:

1 cup instant rice
3 bsp dried cranberries
2 Tbsp dried mixed vegetable blend or freeze-dried vegetables
1 tsp dried parsley
1 tsp diced dried onion
1 tsp granulated garlic
5 ounce can chicken

Directions:

Bring to a boil in your pot 1 1/4 cups water and chicken, with any broth. Add dry ingredients, stir well, tightly cover and let sit for 15 minutes.

Fluff up, and salt to taste if desired.

Creamy Chicken and Mushroom Rice

In a sandwich bag:

1 cup instant rice, white or brown
5 Tbsp dry cream of mushroom soup mix*
1 Tbsp crumbled dried mushrooms

Also take:

5 ounce can of chicken breast

Directions:

Bring 1 1/4 cups water and chicken, with any broth, to boil in your pot. Add in rice mixture and stir well.

Take off heat, cover tightly and let sit for 10 minutes. Stir well.

Note:

Find the recipe for dry cream of mushroom soup mix in the Dry Mixes section.

Sweet N' Salty Chicken Trasherole

In a sandwich bag:

2 cups instant rice

Also take:

7 ounce pouch chicken
2 packets broth concentrate
2 packets olive or coconut oil
4 packets honey
1 single serving bag kettle style potato chips

Directions:

Add 2 cups water, chicken, broth concentrate, oil and honey to your pot, bring to a boil. Stir in rice, cover tightly and take off stove, let sit for 10 minutes.

Gently crush the potato chips through the bag (if at high altitude, open bag first). Stir meal, divide between pot and a bag, bowl, or cup for second serving, and top with chips. If desired, drizzle a bit more honey on top.

Serves 2.

Warm Chicken Curry Rice Salad

In a sandwich bag:

2 cups instant rice
1/2 cup toasted sunflower seeds or hemp seeds
1/4 cup diced dried apple
2 Tbsp diced dried celery or celery flakes
1 Tbsp diced dried carrot

Also take:

7 ounce pouch of chicken

Dressing:

Mix together in a leak proof container:

1/4 cup olive oil
1 tsp brown sugar
1/2 tsp granulated garlic
1 tsp curry powder
1/2 tsp ground cumin
Pinch of sea salt

Directions:

Bring 2 1/4 cups water and the chicken to a boil in your pot. Stir in the dry ingredients; turn off the heat and let sit tightly covered for 15 minutes.

Shake the dressing well, and toss with the rice.

Serves 2

Orange Chicken Rice

In a sandwich bag:

2 cups instant rice
1/2 cup freeze-dried oranges
2 Tbsp shredded coconut
1 Tbsp diced dried onion
Pinch red pepper flakes

Also take:

5 ounce can chicken
2 packets chicken broth concentrate
1 Tbsp coconut aminos

Directions:

Bring 2 1/2 cups water, chicken, broth concentrate, and aminos to a boil in your pot.

Add in the dry ingredients and turn off the stove. Stir well, tightly cover and let sit for 15 minutes.

Fluff up before serving.

Serves 2

Pineapple and Chicken Curry

In a snack bag:

1/2 cup dried pineapple chunks
2 Tbsp diced dried red bell pepper
2 Tbsp diced dried onion
1/4 tsp diced dried jalapeño
1/2 tsp dried garlic

Also take:

1 tsp mild curry powder (in small bag)
1 Tbsp or 1 packet vegetable oil
7 ounce pouch chicken
1 mini "airline size" bottle of rum

In a quart freezer bag:

2 cups instant rice

Directions:

Cover the dried vegetables and fruit with 1/2 cup cool water and let sit for 15 minutes. Drain off any remaining water.

Meanwhile, open the chicken pouch and pour the rum in, let sit.

Add 2 cups water near boiling water to the rice, stir, seal tightly and put in a cozy for 15 minutes.

In your pot heat the oil over medium heat and cook the vegetables and curry powder for a couple minutes till hot. Lower the flame, add the chicken and heat through. Divide the rice and top with the sauce.

Serves 2

Rice and Tomato Chicken Pilaf

In a sandwich bag:

1 cup instant white rice
2 Tbsp diced sun-dried tomatoes
1 Tbsp tomato powder
1 Tbsp diced dried onion
1/4 teaspoon dried thyme
1/4 tsp ground black pepper
1/4 tsp fine sea salt

Also take:

7 ounce pouch chicken breast
1 Tbsp or 1 packet olive oil

Directions:

Bring the chicken, oil and 1 1/4 cups water to a boil in your pot.

Turn off the stove and add in the dry ingredients.

Stir well, cover tightly and let sit for 15 minutes.

Serves 1 to 2

Sweet and Sour Chicken over Rice

In a snack bag:

1/4 cup diced dried chewy sweetened pineapple
1 Tbsp diced candied ginger
1 Tbsp diced dried bell peppers
1 Tbsp dried celery flakes
1 tsp cornstarch or arrowroot
1/4 tsp dried garlic

In a quart freezer bag:

1 1/2 cups instant rice (or dehydrated Jasmine rice)

Also take:

7 ounce package chicken

In a leak proof bottle:

3 Tbsp unseasoned rice vinegar
1 Tbsp coconut aminos
1 Tbsp honey

Bring 1 1/2 cups water to a near boil, add it to the rice bag. Seal tightly and put in a cozy for 15 minutes.

Meanwhile in your pot combine the dry ingredients with 3/4 cup water. Shake up the liquid sauce in the bottle and add in. Bring to a boil stirring often. Lower the heat to low and add in the chicken. Heat through.

Serve the sauce over the rice.

Serves 2

Chicken with Brown Rice

In a sandwich bag:

1 1/2 cups instant brown rice
1/2 cup freeze-dried green peas
1/2 tsp diced dried garlic
1/4 tsp ground black pepper

Also take:
5 ounce can or 7 ounce pouch chicken breast
2 packets chicken broth concentrate
1 Tbsp or 1 packet olive oil

Directions:

Bring the chicken with any broth, broth concentrate, oil and 1 1/2 cups water to a boil in your pot. Add in the dry ingredients. Cover tightly and let sit for 15 minutes.

Serves 1 to 2

Saffron Chicken Rice

In a sandwich bag:

1 cup cooked and dehydrated Jasmine rice
1 Tbsp diced dried onion
1/2 tsp ground cardamom
1/8 tsp ground saffron
Pinch of cayenne pepper

Also take:

1 Tbsp or 1 packet extra virgin olive oil
1 packet chicken broth concentrate
5 ounce can chicken

Directions:

Bring 1 cup water, oil, broth concentrate, and the chicken to a boil.

Add in the dry ingredients. Stir well, cover tightly and let sit for 15 minutes.

Serves 1

Pasta

Chicken Ramen

In a sandwich bag:

3 ounce rice ramen package, discard flavor packet
1/4 cup freeze-dried or dehydrated canned chicken
1/4 cup freeze-dried green peas
1 Tbsp dried carrot powder

Also take:

1 packet chicken broth concentrate

Directions:

Bring 1 1/2 cups water to a boil and add in the dry ingredients.

Stir well and cook gently for 3 minutes.

Take off the stove and let sit tightly covered for a couple minutes.

Serves 1

Chicken Primavera Ramen

In a sandwich bag:

3 ounce rice ramen package, discard flavor packet
1/4 cup freeze-dried zucchini
2 Tbsp freeze-dried or dehydrated canned chicken
2 Tbsp tomato powder
1 Tbsp diced freeze-dried or dehydrated celery
1 Tbsp freeze-dried or dehydrated bell pepper
1 tsp Italian herb

Also take:

1 packet chicken broth concentrate

Directions:

Bring 1 1/2 cups water to a boil and add in the dry ingredients. Stir well and cook gently for 3 minutes.

Take off the stove and let sit tightly covered for a couple minutes.

Serves 1

Hearty Beef and Veggie Noodles

In a sandwich bag:

3 ounce rice ramen package, discard flavor packet
1/4 cup freeze dried roast beef cubes
1 Tbsp dried carrots
1 Tbsp dried onions
1 tsp dried chives
1/8 tsp red pepper flakes

Also take:

1 packet beef broth concentrate
1 tsp coconut aminos

Directions:

Bring 1 1/2 cups water and coconut aminos to a boil, add in the dry ingredients. Stir well and cook gently for 3 minutes.

Take off the stove and let sit tightly covered for a couple minutes.

Serves 1

Sesame Noodles

In a snack size bag:

1/2 cup diced dried carrots
1/4 cup dried or freeze-dried green peas

In a sandwich bag:

8 ounces gluten-free spaghetti, broken in half

In a leak-proof bottle:
2 Tbsp coconut aminos
2 tsp sesame oil
2 tsp rice wine vinegar
1/4 tsp red pepper flakes
1/4 tsp granulated garlic
1/4 tsp sugar

Also take:

5 ounce can or 7 ounce pouch chicken

Directions:

Add the vegetable bag and 6 cups water to a 2 liter pot, bring to a boil.

Add in pasta, cook for time on package, drain carefully.

Toss with chicken (and any broth), shake up sauce and stir in.

Serves 2

Spicy Chicken Spaghetti

In a sandwich bag:

4 ounces gluten-free spaghetti, broken into quarters
3 Tbsp dried mushrooms
1 Tbsp dried carrots
1 Tbsp dried onion
1/4 tsp diced dried garlic
1/4 tsp red pepper flakes

Also take:

5 ounce can or 7 ounce pouch of chicken
1 packet chicken broth concentrate
4 tsp coconut aminos

Add 1 1/2 cups water, the chicken, and pasta bag ingredients into your pot. Bring to a boil, put the lid on and turn down to low. Let it gently bubble for cooking time on pasta package.

Stir a couple times to keep the pasta moving.

Turn off the heat and add coconut aminos.

Serves 1 to 2 (A very hungry hiker could eat the whole recipe, normal appetites two.)

Garden Marinara

In a sandwich bag:

6 ounces gluten-free pasta shapes
2 Tbsp dried mushrooms
1/4 cup freeze-dried mixed vegetables

In a pint freezer bag:

1/4 cup tomato powder
1/2 tsp Italian seasoning
1/2 tsp sugar
1/4 tsp diced dried garlic
1/4 tsp ground black pepper
Pinch of salt

Directions:

Bring 5 cups water to a boil in your pot. Take out 1 cup of it. Slowly add water to the tomato mix. Stir till sauce reaches the texture you like, you will need at least 3/4 cup water; adding more will produce a thinner sauce. Seal the bag tightly and set aside.

Meanwhile, add the pasta and vegetables to the rest of the water in the pot. Boil gently for time on pasta package. Turn off heat and drain carefully. Add the prepared sauce, Parmesan cheese and if desired, a drizzle of olive oil. Toss together.

Serves 2

Herbed Chicken Pasta

In a sandwich bag:

8 ounces gluten-free angel hair or spaghetti (break in thirds)

In a snack bag:

1 Tbsp dried parsley
1 Tbsp dried chives
1 tsp dry celery flakes
1 tsp granulated garlic
1/8 tsp ground black pepper
Pinch of red pepper flakes

Also take:

1 Tbsp or 1 packet olive oil
7 ounce pouch chicken

Directions:

Add the dry pasta to 4 cups water and bring to a boil in your pot. Cook for time on pasta package. Turn off the heat and drain the water off carefully.

Toss with the oil, herbs, chicken and spices. If desired, heat through on very low heat for a minute or two.

Serves 2.

Fall Harvest pasta

In a sandwich bag:

8 ounces gluten-free small pasta shapes
1/4 cup dried mushrooms
1/4 cup freeze-dried hamburger

In a snack bag:

1/2 tsp dried diced garlic
1/4 cup hemp seeds
1 1/2 tsp dry parsley

Also take:

1/4 cup or 4 packets olive oil

Directions:

Bring 3 cups water to a boil in your pot. Add the pasta bag contents and cook for time on pasta package. Turn off the heat and drain carefully.

Toss the pasta with the seasonings and oil.

Serves 2

Apricot and Rosemary Pasta

In a sandwich bag:

8 ounces gluten-free small pasta shapes

In a snack bag:

1 cup diced dried apricots
1 tsp dried rosemary, crumbled
1 tsp diced dried garlic

Also take:

2 Tbsp or 2 Packets olive oil
3/4 cup dry white wine

Also take:

Ground black pepper and salt, to taste

Directions:

Bring to boil 6 cups water in a 2 liter pot. Cook pasta for time on package drain and set aside in a new freezer bag or in a bowl.

Heat the oil in your pot and add the garlic, rosemary and apricots. Heat through and add in the wine. Bring to a simmer and toss with the cooked pasta. Add pepper and salt to taste.

Serves 2

Notes: You can find wine often in small servings, in shelf stable packaging. These packages keep the wine fresh and flatten down after using. If you are not a wine drinker, substitute broth.

Pasta Primavera

In a sandwich bag:

4 ounces pre cooked and dehydrated gluten-free pasta shapes
1/4 cup freeze-dried mixed vegetables

Also take:

1 Tbsp or 1 packet olive oil
1 Tbsp Italian seasoning
Fine sea salt

Directions:

Boil 2 cups water, add in the pasta and vegetables. Cover and let sit for 5 minutes. Drain carefully.

Toss the oil and seasoning with the pasta. Add salt to taste.

Serves 1

Veggie and Pasta Toss

In a sandwich bag:

4 ounces of precooked and dehydrated gluten-free pasta shapes
1/4 cup of sun dried tomatoes, minced
2 Tbsp dried broccoli
1/4 tsp granulated garlic

Also take:

1 Tbsp or 1 packet olive oil
1 Tbsp hemp seeds
Fine sea salt

Directions:

Bring to a boil 2 cups water, add in the pasta and vegetables. Let sit covered for 5 minutes.

Drain excess water carefully. Add in the oil, hemp seeds and salt to taste.

Serves 1

Rustic Pasta

In a sandwich bag:

8 ounces small gluten-free pasta shapes

In a snack size bag:

2 Tbsp hulled hemp seeds
1 Tbsp dried basil
1 tsp granulated garlic

Also take:

2 packets or 2 Tbsp olive oil
4.3 ounce bag shelf stable crumbled bacon

Directions:

Bring a 2 liter pot half filled with water to boil. Add in pasta, cook for time on package, lowering flame so it doesn't boil over.

Drain carefully, leaving about a Tablespoon water behind. Add in oil, seasoning bag, and half the bacon. Stir till coated.

Serves 2

Note:

Use the remaining bacon the next morning or afternoon in a meal.

Snacks and Desserts

3 Ingredient Seed Butter Balls

Ingredients:

2 Tbsp gluten-free rolled oats
2 Tbsp seed butter of choice
2 tsp raw honey

Directions:

Whirl the oats in a blender till finely ground.

Add the seed butter and honey to a mixing bowl, work in the oat flour.

Mix well with a spoon and form into small balls.

Store in an airtight container or a plastic bag.

Note:

If your seed butter isn't salted, add in a pinch of fine sea salt.

Seed & Chocolate Balls

Ingredients:

1/2 cup seed butter of choice
3 Tbsp cocoa powder + more for rolling
3 Tbsp coconut sugar
2 Tbsp dairy-free mini chocolate chips
1 tsp pure vanilla extract

Directions:

Mix all the ingredients in a medium bowl.

Scoop out balls (any size) of the mix and drop in a bowl of extra cocoa powder.

Roll gently to cover and tap to knock off extra back in the bowl.

Store tightly covered in the refrigerator till trail time.

Carry in a small plastic box to protect.

Seed and Granola Balls

Ingredients:

1/3 cup raw honey
1/4 cup seed butter
2 Tbsp coconut oil
1 cup crispy rice cereal
1 cup gluten-free rolled oats
1/4 cup diced dried fruit

Directions:

In a saucepan over medium heat, warm up the honey, seed butter, and coconut oil. Stir until melted and smooth, a couple minutes.

Remove from the heat; stir in cereal, oats, and dried fruit.

Drop mixture by spoonfuls onto a parchment paper lined baking sheet. Let set up for an hour and then store tightly covered in the refrigerator till trail time.

Carry in a small plastic box to protect.

Sunballs

Ingredients:

1/2 cup quick cooking gluten-free oats
1/2 cup oat flour
1/2 tsp ground cinnamon
1/4 cup dried cherries
1/4 cup sunflower spread
1/4 cup raw honey
1 Tbsp organic powdered sugar

Directions:

Mix the oats through honey together in a medium mixing bowl. Make balls with a 1 tablespoon disher, packing tightly with hands and rolling into balls.

Add powdered sugar to a shallow bowl, roll balls in sugar. Store balls in an airtight container, in the refrigerator.

To carry on trail, carry balls in a freezer bag, rolled up, protected from crushing, such as in a drinking cup.

Makes about 14 balls.

Notes:

You can make your own oat flour, grind oats in a blender.

Read powdered sugar labels. Some contain tapioca starch, others cornstarch. I have good luck with Wholesome Sweeteners organic brand.

Sunflower Bars

Ingredients:

1 1/2 cups golden raisins
1 cup sunflower seeds
1/4 tsp fine sea salt

Directions:

Heat a large skillet over medium heat, and dry toast the sunflower seeds, stirring often, until golden and smelling good. Take off heat, let cool a bit.

Line a 9×5 bread pan with plastic wrap, with enough extra for an overhang on each side.

Add the sunflower seeds, raisins and salt in a food processor, process until finely ground, scraping the sides as needed.

Drop into the prepared pan, spreading out a bit (it is sticky). Fold the overhang over, gently press down to spread it evenly, then pack with your palms tightly.

Chill overnight, remove and cut into bars. Wrap each bar, store in a tightly sealed container.

Sunflower & Cherry No Bake Bars

Ingredients:

2 cups gluten-free rolled oats
1 cup sunflower seeds
1 cup dried cherries
1 cup sunflower butter
3/4 cup pure maple syrup
2 Tbsp coconut oil
1 tsp ground cinnamon
1/2 tsp fine sea salt

Directions:

Preheat oven to 350°, spread oats and sunflower seeds on a large rimmed baking sheet. Bake for 10 minutes, till oats are toasted and turning golden. Let cool and mix with cherries in a large mixing bowl.

Meanwhile, add Sunbutter, maple syrup, coconut oil, cinnamon and sea salt to a small saucepan. Heat over medium for 10 minutes, until bubbling. Take off heat, stir until smooth. Pour over oats, work in with a spatula.

Spread oat mixture into an oiled 11×8 pan (I used a rimmed quarter size baking sheet), pressing down firmly.

Chill for at least 2 hours, then cut into bars. Store tightly sealed in refrigerator.

Allergy Friendly Chocolate Covered Cherry Granola Bars

Ingredients:

2 1/2 cups crisp rice cereal (see notes)
1 1/2 cups gluten-free old-fashioned oats
1/2 cup dried cherries
1/2 cup dairy-free chocolate chips
3/4 cup sunflower butter
1/4 cup raw honey
1/4 cup pure maple syrup
1/4 cup brown sugar, packed

Directions:

Spray or lightly oil a 9×13" pan. Line with parchment paper cut to fit bottom of pan, and up the end sides. Spray or oil the paper.

Mix the cereal, oats, cherries and chocolate chips together in a large bowl.

Add the sunflower butter, honey, maple syrup and brown sugar to a medium mixing bowl, heat in microwave for 1 minute on high. Remove and stir until smooth.

Add to dry mix, stir till thoroughly combined with a silicone spatula. Pack into prepared pan, pressing down evenly.

Let cool for an hour, cut with a sharp knife into bars. Wrap each bar individually. For best storage, keep in refrigerator or freezer until snack time.

Notes:

On crisp rice cereal, I have found the store brands to be safer than the name brand – mostly due to the ingredient list. Does one need high fructose corn syrup in it? No. So read the labels, you might find the generic looks better as well.

Simmered Cherries

In a sandwich bag:

6 ounces dried tart cherries
6 Tbsp coconut sugar
3 Tbsp instant tapioca
1/2 tsp True Lemon or Lime powder (2 packets)
1/2 tsp ground cinnamon

Directions:

Add the dry ingredients to your pot with 2 cups water and let sit for 15 minutes to soak.

Bring to a boil and cook for a minute.

Take off the stove and cool in a snow bank or a cold stream. It will thicken as it cools.

Serves 2 to 4

Note:

Add an airline size bottle rum after boiling for an adult treat.

Applesauce

In a sandwich bag:

1 cup dried chopped apples
1/4 cup brown or coconut sugar
1/4 cup raisins
1/2 tsp ground cinnamon
1/4 tsp ground nutmeg
Pinch fine sea salt

Directions:

Add the ingredients to your pot, cover with water and bring to a boil.

Take off the stove and let sit tightly covered for 5 minutes.

Serves 2 to 4

Cranberry Pear Compote

Ingredients:

1/4 cup dried cranberries
1/4 cup dried pears, chopped
2 Tbsp brown sugar
1/4 tsp dried orange zest (or a True Orange packet)
Pinch fine sea salt

At home:

Pack the ingredients in a snack bag.

Bring 1/4 cup water to a boil, add in ingredients. Let hydrate for 10 to 30 minutes. If a bit dry, add in a little more water as needed.

Serves 2.

Homemade Pudding

In a sandwich bag:

1/2 cup powdered coconut milk
1/4 cup sugar
3 Tbsp cornstarch
1/2 tsp vanilla powder
1/8 tsp fine sea salt

Also take:

1 Tbsp or 1 packet coconut oil

Directions:

Add the mix and 2 cups cold water to your pot. Using a small whisk stir well while bringing to a boil.

As soon as it boils and is thick, turn off the stove and whisk in the coconut oil.

Serve warm or chill in a snow bank or cold stream.

Serves 2 to 4 depending on appetite

Notes:

Find vanilla powder where coffee/espresso products are sold, or online through gourmet baking supply sites.

For an easy banana pudding add in 2 Tbsp powdered freeze-dried bananas with the dry ingredients and top with gluten-free vanilla cookies.

Rice Pudding

In a sandwich bag:

2/3 cup instant rice
1/3 cup raisins
1/4 cup brown sugar
3 Tbsp powdered coconut milk
1 tsp potato starch
1/4 tsp cinnamon
Pinch fine sea salt

Directions:

Bring 1 cup water to a boil in your pot.

Add in the dry ingredients, stirring well. Turn off the stove and cover tightly and let sit for 10 minutes.

Serves 2 as a desert, 1 for breakfast

Tapioca Pudding

In a sandwich bag:

2/3 cup powdered coconut milk
3 Tbsp instant tapioca
3 Tbsp sugar
1 tsp vanilla powder
1/8 tsp salt

Directions:

Add the dry ingredients to your pot with 2 cups water and let sit for 15 minutes.

Bring to a boil, stirring often and once boiling, cook for a minute.

Take off the stove and stash in a snow bank or cold stream. The pudding will thicken as it cools.

Serves 2

Note:

Find vanilla powder in stores specializing in coffee/espresso bar products. It can also be found online through baking specialty stores. If you cannot find it, use vanilla sugar or vanilla extract.

Blueberry Rice Pudding

In a sandwich bag:

2/3 cup instant rice
1/3 cup dried blueberries
3 Tbsp powdered coconut milk milk
3 Tbsp maple or coconut sugar
2 tsp potato starch
1/2 tsp ground cinnamon
Pinch fine sea salt

Directions:

Bring 1 cup water to a boil in your pot. Add in the dry ingredients, stirring well.

Cover tightly and let sit for 15 minutes.

Serves 1 to 2

Dry Mixes

Tomato leather

Ingredients:

1 small onion, minced
2 garlic cloves, minced
1 Tbsp olive oil
12 ounces tomato paste (unsalted if desired)
1 tsp sugar
2 tsp parsley, chopped or 1 Tbsp dry
Ground black pepper, to taste
1/4 tsp dried basil

Directions:

Sauté onions and garlic in oil until soft and golden. Add remaining ingredients and cook slowly for 10 minutes over medium heat. If bubbling too much, turn to low.

Spread tomato mixture on a parchment paper lined dehydrator tray. Dry at 135-140* for about 6 hours. When dry (pliable but not sticky), let cool on counter.

Freeze for an hour, and then whirl in a blender to powder and store in a tightly sealed plastic bag. It may be frozen for longer storage.

Low Sodium "Faux-Soy Sauce"

Ingredients:

3/4 cup garlic vinegar
3 Tbsp dark molasses
3 tsp onion powder

Directions:

Mix together in a sterilized small mason jar. Store in the refrigerator for up to a month. Makes a shy 1 cup.

Carry in a leak proof container and use when soy sauce is called for in recipes. Use instead of coconut aminos as well.

It adds a nice spike of flavor without sodium or MSG, and is great sprinkled on rice and pasta dishes, or to dip California rolls into.

Salsa Pico De Gallo

At home mix together in a glass bowl:

14 ounce can tomatoes, drained
4 ounce can diced green Chile peppers, drained
3/4 cup chopped onion
1 Tbsp fresh lime juice
1/4 tsp dried diced garlic or 1 large clove diced
3/4 tsp dried oregano
1/4 tsp ground black pepper
3 Tbsp fresh or 3 tsp dry cilantro

Directions:

Process till chunky smooth in a food chopper or blender.

Spread on a parchment paper lined dehydrator tray. Dry at 135* till dry (no sticky or wet spots, it will be like fruit leather.) When dry, either break up, or whirl in a blender to powder if desired.

Recipe makes about 2 cups fresh. When ready to rehydrate start with equal amounts cool water to dried product and add water till desired texture.

A serving size is 1 to 2 Tablespoons of dried mix. Carry it in snack size zip top bags. You can use cold or hot water to rehydrate.

Instant Salsa

In a snack size bag:

1/4 cup diced sun-dried tomatoes
1 Tbsp diced dried shallots or onions
1 Tbsp tomato powder
2 tsp diced dried jalapeños
3 packets True Lime powder
1/2 tsp sugar
1/4 tsp diced dried garlic
1/4 tsp ground pepper
Pinch of sea salt

Directions:

Add 3/4 cup cool water, stirring well and seal tightly. Let sit for 30 minutes to an hour to rehydrate. Knead the bag gently every 10 minutes or so.

Makes 1 cup salsa. This is a considerable amount, you may want to halve the recipe. For spicier salsa up the jalapeños to a Tablespoon. This would work well with part of the tomatoes replaced with diced dried bell peppers or freeze dried mango.

Cranberry Sauce

In a snack bag:

1/4 cup dried sweetened cranberries
2 tsp sugar

Directions:

Combine ingredients and 1/2 cup water in a small pot and bring to a boil. Reduce heat and simmer for about 8 minutes or until the cranberries start looking a little saucy

Note:

It will appear somewhat soupy, but will thicken once cooled. Eat warm or allow to cool for a thicker sauce.

Parma "Cheese" Topper

Ingredients:

1/4 cup nutritional yeast
1/4 cup sesame seeds
1/4 tsp fine sea salt

Directions:

In a blender whirl till combined. Store in a tightly sealed container, in a dry cool place.

Use 1 to 2 Tablespoon as a serving. Sprinkle over dishes instead of Parmesan cheese.

Nutritional Yeast Free Vegetable Broth Mix

Ingredients:

1 Tbsp onion powder
1 Tbsp dried celery flakes
1 Tbsp dried parsley flakes
1 1/2 tsp granulated garlic
1/2 tsp fine sea salt
1/2 tsp ground savory
1/2 tsp dried marjoram
1/2 tsp dried thyme
1/4 tsp pepper
1/4 tsp turmeric powder
1/4 tsp ground sage

Directions:

Combine all ingredients in a small bowl, cover tightly and shake to mix. Store in an airtight container. Shake well before using. For a smooth powder, whirl in a blender.

Use in place of vegetable bouillon or broth concentrate, or to add flavor to many recipes. Use 1 tablespoon mix per cup of water.

Makes 1/4 cup

Note:

This recipe does not contain nutritional yeast for those affected by it.

Vegan Friendly Broth Powder

Ingredients:

1 1/3 cups Large Flake Nutritional Yeast
2 Tbsp onion powder (not onion salt!)
1 Tbsp granulated garlic
1 tsp dried thyme
1 tsp dried rubbed sage
1 tsp paprika
1/2 tsp ground turmeric
1/2 tsp dried parsley
1/4 tsp celery seed

Directions:

Add the ingredients in a high-speed blender. Process on high until smooth (takes less than 30 seconds).

Store in an airtight container.

Use 1 Tablespoon dry mix per cup of water.

Makes about 12 Tablespoons dry mix.

Brown Gravy Mix

Ingredients:

1 2/3 cups cornstarch
6 tablespoons lower sodium beef bouillon powder (or vegan broth recipe)
4 tsp instant coffee or espresso powder
2 tsp onion powder
1 tsp granulated garlic
1/2 tsp ground black pepper
1/2 tsp paprika

Directions:

Combine all ingredients in an airtight container. With lid on tightly, shake to blend.

To make gravy, measure 3 Tablespoons mix and pack in a small bag. Add 1 1/2 cups cool water to the mix in your pot. Bring to a boil and simmer 1 minute, stirring till thick.

Makes 10 batches of gravy mix

Vegan Dry Cream of Mushroom Soup Mix

Ingredients:

½ cup powdered coconut milk
3 Tbsp potato starch or cornstarch
2 Tbsp dried shiitake mushrooms, crumbled
1 Tbsp veggie broth mix
1 1/2 tsp dried parsley
1/2 tsp onion powder
1/4 tsp dried thyme
1/4 tsp dried basil
1/4 tsp fine sea salt
1/8 tsp ground black pepper

Directions:

Combine in a glass mason jar, seal and shake well. Makes about 10 Tablespoons, or 2 batches worth.

Shake before using.

To make soup:

Add 5 Tablespoons mix to 1 cup water, heat over a low flame till thickened, whisking preferably, constantly.

Spicy Sunflower Sauce

Ingredients:

1/3 cup sunflower butter
2 Tbsp plain rice vinegar
1 Tbsp coconut aminos
2 tsp lemon juice
1 tsp toasted sesame oil
1/2 tsp granulated garlic
1/4 tsp onion powder
1/4 tsp red pepper flakes
1 to 2 Tbsp Thai sweet chili sauce

Directions:

Stir ingredients until smooth. Carry in a tightly sealed container or small bag.

If carrying on trail, use first day.

Cheezy Hemp Seed Sauce

Ingredients:

1/2 cup hemp seeds
2 Tbsp cornstarch or arrowroot/potato starch
1 tsp granulated garlic
1/2 tsp onion powder
1/2 tsp ground black pepper
1/2 tsp fine sea salt
2 Tbsp powdered coconut milk

Directions:

At home combine ingredients in a blender, whirl until seeds are finely chopped. Store in a mason jar tightly sealed, in the refrigerator, until trip time.

Pack sauce into a snack bag, seal tightly. Also take 4 tablespoon coconut oil (In warm temperatures carry in a leak-proof bottle).

To prepare:

Melt the coconut oil in a cooking pot, over a low flame.

Add in 1 1/2 cups water, and bring to a boil.

Lower the flame as low as it can go, add in dry sauce mix and whisk (with a mini whisk or fork/spork) until sauce is thickened.

Remove from heat. Serve over desired carb, such as 8 ounces (dry weight) gluten-free pasta cooked separately, or instant rice or quinoa.

About The Authors

Sarah and Matthew live in a town in the foothills of Mt. Rainier, in Washington State.

Sarah is the author of Freezer Bag Cooking: Trail Food Made Simple, Trail Eats, Trail Cooking: Trail Food Made Gourmet, Freezer Bag Cooking: Adventure Ready Recipes, Oats Gone Wild and Natural Body Care.

Find us online at www.trailcooking.com

HIKING FREE	**1**
ALLERGY FRIENDLY RECIPES FOR THE OUTDOORS	1
HIKING FREE	**2**
THE BACK STORY	3
COOKING & GEAR METHODS	5
THE RECIPES	8
DRINKS	9
BREAKFAST	31
LUNCH	54
DINNER	61
SOUP	62
RICE DISHES	75
PASTA	88
SNACKS AND DESSERTS	101
DRY MIXES	116
ABOUT THE AUTHORS	129

Made in the
USA
Columbia, SC